971
.316
You

9855

Young, Peter, 1949-
   The Kee to Bala is Dunn's Pavilion / by Peter Young.
--Oshawa, Ont. : PDA Communications, c1997.
  67 p. : ill.

877814   ISBN:0968195105 (pbk.)

1. Kee to Bala (Dance hall) - History. 2. Dance
orchestras - Ontario - Bala - History. 3. Bala

(SEE NEXT CARD)

94   98MAR17   3559/he   1-511475

THE
KEE TO BALA

is

DUNN'S PAVILION

by Peter Young

Published by: PDA Communications Ltd.
                 76 Hillcroft Street
                 Oshawa, Ontario, Canada
                 L1G 2L2

Canadian Cataloguing in Publication Data:

Young, Peter, 1949 -
The Kee To Bala Is Dunn's Pavilion

ISBN 0-9681951-0-5

1. Kee to Bala (Dance hall) - History. 2. Dance orchestra - Ontario
- Bala - History. 3. Bala (Ont.) - History.
I. Title

FC3099.B328Z57 1997   971.3'16   C97-930646-9
F1059.5.B34Y68 1997

Preface

There was a time in Ontario when the May 24th long weekend was the traditional opening date for most of Ontario's dance pavilions. During this annual salute to summer's pending arrival, wooden shutters would be raised, the dance floor was lovingly polished until it gleamed in preparation for another season of dancing feet, the refreshment booth was stocked up and posters were distributed throughout cottage country announcing the season's attractions.

Unfortunately, with the exception of a few notable venues such as The Kee to Bala, none of these wonderful dance pavilions are operating today. Yet the memories of warm summer evenings, great music, dancing and romance are very dear to the hearts of many people, and I felt that a book on the subject would be well received.

Between 1994 and 1996 I travelled extensively throughout Ontario, researching this province's rich history of dance pavilions and dancehalls. I interviewed hundreds of people and have received letters and photographs from hundreds more. Former pavilion owners, musicians and the general public have fondly recalled their dancing years, from the memorable Big Band era well into the more recent years of rock 'n' roll.

After completing this research, I wrote a comprehensive book chronicling every well known dancehall, as well as several of the lesser known spots throughout the province. The book is called "Come Dancing - A Celebration of Ontario's Dance Pavilions." Due to the length of time it is requiring to bring such a large project to the actual finished book form, I decided to publish a smaller work about a single pavilion in the meantime that could be brought to market quickly. In order to determine which dancehall should be featured, I asked myself a question: What location in Ontario best represents the subject of dance pavilions in this province?

Without hesitation, Dunn's Pavilion/The Kee to Bala came to mind.

This notable Muskoka dance pavilion has been cherished by thousands of people who have danced here to bands ranging from The Varsity Collegians to The Dorsey Brothers to Louis Armstrong to Frank Evans to Lighthouse to Kim Mitchell.

During its long life, Dunn's Pavilion/The Kee to Bala has featured just about every form of dance and concert music one could wish for. (Perhaps with the exception of opera!)

I would like to thank the many people who have granted interviews and sent me letters sharing your thoughts and memories about Dunn's Pavilion/The Kee to Bala - you have made this book possible. Although all contributors are mentioned by name throughout this text, I would like to give particular thanks to Don and Winnifred McIndoe, the house photographers at Dunn's for many years. Don kindly allowed me to make copies of many of his precious photos for use in this book. All photo credits are noted at the end of the book.

Please keep in mind that when people are recalling the past, some facts such as names, dates and other details may be a little hazy. Remember that we are going back to the 1920's, when the story of Dunn's begins. In many cases I have asked people to recall a time of their life that took place over 50 years ago - most of us find it difficult to remember what we had for supper last Thursday! I hope you are anxious to enjoy the book for the memories, and hopefully, to refresh in your own mind the wonderful times that you personally experienced dancing at Muskoka's most popular pavilion:
Dunn's Pavilion. The Kee to Bala.

Peter Young

Dunn's Pavilion.

The Kee To Bala

6

Introduction

"If you build it, they will come."

Long before the fictional movie Field of Dreams - where a farmer upon hearing a voice speaking to him, creates a baseball diamond in the middle of a field of corn - Gerry Patrick Dunn felt the same real-life urge to push ahead in 1941 with an idea so grandiose it left some people scratching their heads in amazement. Gerry erected the most ambitious dance pavilion ever built in Ontario cottage country.

It was to become the province's most successful summer dance venue: Dunn's Pavilion.

"Where All Muskoka Dances"

When it was completed and opened its doors for business in the summer of 1942 there may still have been a few pessimists who felt the pavilion would never fly, but they were by far a minority. Gerry's gift to Bala was a treasure that attracted dancers from near and far, who dressed in their finest attire to dance in an atmosphere that was first-class all the way. The new pavilion was an immediate hit with everyone, featuring dancing six nights a week throughout the summer, with at least one major Big Band attraction coming in every week for an engagement.

It was unheard of in the 1940's for famous entertainers to travel so far away from their traditional touring routes, but Dunn's Pavilion soon earned the enviable reputation in the music industry as one of the premier summer dancehalls in Canada in which to play.

"Plus, I was able to offer them mid-week employment," chuckles Gerry. "The big bands had no trouble playing halls on weekend nights, and I always had a full house on weekends with my regular house bands, so it worked out well - they were happy with the work and I could promise them a good crowd on a Tuesday or Wednesday night."

"Good crowds" may have been an understatement, but it wasn't just the music that attracted thousands of people for a night they'd never forget. Gerry instinctively knew the secret to creating a good business, long before he built his hall. The real estate industry's cliché - location, location, location - certainly contributed to the pavilion's prosperity, but it was Gerry's personal charm and attentiveness to every detail that ensured Dunn's Pavilion would enjoy a long run in Bala. He was more than a gracious host - he made every person feel special, greeting them personally at the door. And once inside the pavilion, long before the band played its first note, the unique decor of the hall convinced patrons that for that evening they were about as far away from cottage land as their minds would allow them to travel - perhaps Miami, somewhere in California, or even the south seas.

Little did Gerry know at the time he built the pavilion on Lake Muskoka, that for over five decades, the tradition he began would continue every summer. Oh, there have been a succession of owners since Gerry; some have enjoyed the rewards of good management, others have been not much more than caretakers, while another operator lost his shirt.

But Dunn's Pavilion, which for nearly 30 years has been called The Kee to Bala, continues to draw thousands of people who attend dances with one intention: to have a good time, just like their parents and their grandparents did in their own way in previous years. Tank tops and blue jeans have long ago replaced long dresses and sports jackets as acceptable dress wear, the Big Band music of yesterday has given way to rock 'n' roll and BYOB is no longer necessary with The Kee now being fully licensed. But the tradition Gerry Dunn started with his pavilion in 1942 for his generation, repeats itself year after year as new generations of young people discover the musical shrine Gerry conceived.

Gerry Dunn

I feel very fortunate to have been able to interview Gerry Dunn, meeting with him in the summer of 1994 at his Acton Island summer home, located on his beloved Lake Muskoka. Gerry lives on Acton Island from May to October. For 45 years he has travelled to Florida for the winter months,

but the previous winter was the first he stayed at his home in Toronto. He is well into his 90's, and was still driving his auto and taking his boat out on Lake Muskoka regularly. Gerry was good friends with long-term fellow summer Muskokan, Gordon Sinclair, and several other well-known Muskoka people, many of whom have since passed away.

Gerry's cottage, which he designed himself, is located on seven acres of prime Muskoka lakefront which he purchased from the janitor at his dance pavilion in the early 1960's, just before he sold the business. It is a square structure built over the water with a protected two-slip boathouse located underneath the living quarters. A wide balcony wraps around half of the cottage with a large dock below. Plate glass windows surround the three sides overlooking the water, giving a person the feeling of spaciousness and the illusion of floating on a large boat. The continual lapping of water underneath the cottage contributes to the sensation of riding the waves.

And while we are on the topic of waves, Gerry has three boats - one is a regular covered fibreglass runabout, but the other two are Muskoka masterpieces - polished mahogany in-board motorboats, heavily laden with gleaming chrome and brass. The more luxurious of the two has placed first in wooden boat pageants held in the area each summer.

Gerry has always been a designer. He has an extensive workshop at home where he has built furniture and many other wooden projects; he also has a fully stocked work bench in his boathouse. Gerry's talent for envisioning an idea and then carrying through with the plan is best exemplified in the pavilion itself where he brought his dream to reality without the aid of blueprints.

"I was a pharmacist, graduating from the University of Toronto in 1927," says Gerry. "Although I could have gone on to medical school at McGill on a hockey scholarship, the chance came up to purchase Langdon's Ice Cream Parlour in Bala in 1929. My dad had good friends in Bala, but I hadn't ever been to the village. After I bought the store - I paid $11,000 for it - I could see there was great potential for the area to open up with a new road going through some time in the future, and could see that the store and the open-air dance pavilion in the rear, could be a pretty good business opportunity."

L-R back: Mr. Langdon, Reginald Thompson, Chuck Lyon, Mr. Langdon, Norm Amer, Douglas Thompson, Clark Thompson. Seated: Fanny Thompson, Madelaine Thompson, Grace Thompson, Embleton, ?,?.

Kay Thompson sent a photo of several of her future in-laws posing in front of the dancehall/drug store before Gerry purchased the business. The year was 1925, and the name of the store was Langdon's. Kay says the two gents in white shirts and ties are Langdon family members; the others are identified under the picture.

"I needed money to pay for my business and to help it grow," explains Gerry, adding that a summer enterprise allowed him the cold weather months to earn extra income. "So I lived in Detroit in the winter, working at a pharmacy during the day and playing hockey at night." This arrangement lasted a few years and helped Gerry pay off the initial investment he made in the store and dance platform.

"Langdon hired a piano player to play music for dancers on Saturday nights," says Gerry. "When I took over, I changed the music format to that of orchestras, bringing in two university bands - Jerry Richardson and the Varsity Collegians, and Carl Mueller's Varsity Entertainers." Gerry felt the customers were too serious. "They'd sit on chairs around the tables and listen, but not get up and dance. Of course, admission was free at the time - all you had to do was walk through my drug store and out the back to the dance pavilion."

The drug store portion of the business was very lucrative,

bringing in as much money as the dancehall did every season. "People have always assumed that the dance pavilion was my main income, but the store did just as well," says Gerry. There was a long lunch counter/soda fountain, pharmacy items and a large variety of clothing, fishing equipment and hardware stock. Dunn's Drug Store was the only pharmacy between Gravenhurst and Parry Sound, however this business was also seasonal, closing down with the dancehall after the summer ended.

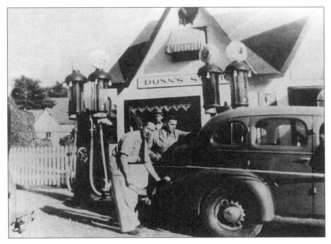

Gerry Dunn working at his gas station, next to the store & pavilion.

Remembering the Original Pavilion

During the second year of ownership, Gerry made the first of three enlargements to the pavilion's 35-foot square dance floor. The structure was eventually covered in completely when the floor had been lengthened to 100 feet.

George Allison recalls in his letter some of the early days on the original dance platform. "Dunn's was the old dark green pavilion-type clapboard and lattice place with the drug store and souvenir area in front and Gerry Dunn always present in white shirt, tie and smart slacks, greeting and welcoming folks (nothing new about Wal-Mart).

"We teens rowed the skiff or canoe to the dock by Dunn's

Pavilion after lunch to meet, have ice cream sodas, dance to the resident jukebox and try to make dates for the evening or for swims the next afternoon.

"In the evenings people came from quite a distance, by road and by water, especially if a known big band was playing. Some of the launches you now see at Antique Boat Shows came loaded with the more affluent young adults, and tied up at the pavilion dock. They went home after the dance through the dark nights with nothing but their red and green navigational lights, and some came to grief from lapsed memories of the shallow rocks, and some from the `affluence of incohol.'

"One frantic summer - my 15th - I spent with my older sister teaching me to waltz and fox-trot so I could attend the Bala Regatta Dance at Dunn's. At that time, whole families went and sat at the ice cream parlour tables and chairs beside the dance floor and watched and listened to the resident band, usually five or six pieces, always with a comedian bass player called `Slap.' I asked a young girl who came from Pittsburgh, Marjorie Smart, staying in a cottage up the shore. We went in the rowboat which was rough, rowing in a blazer, shirt, tie and grey flannels. She had a black dress trimmed in white and was stunning. My parents drove while I rowed and brought my sister, who glared at me to do the correct steps. During the evening they had a waltz competition and - that's right - Marjorie and I won. The prizes were a matching black enamel-on-gold cigarette case and heart-shaped compact, each engraved `Bala Regatta Dance 1936.' As summer romances usually go, I never saw Marjorie again after she went to school that fall.

"Later, the travelling big bands were the highlight of the summer dances. On our honeymoon we went to dance to Les Brown in the `new' Dunn's. There was no liquor sold so it was BYOB in a plain paper bag or satchel. That was when we learned it took ten empty bottles from under the tables to get a one-ounce drink from the dregs, if you ran out."

Leone (Palmer) Fisher also writes about the fun to be found at Dunn's long before the famous pavilion was constructed: "About 1937 to '45 my sister Frances and I had a glorious time in summers staying at a cottage at Dudley, three miles north of Bala. Of course we would walk or perhaps canoe, into Dunn's. At first it was just a dance floor (not over the water then) and afternoons we danced to a jukebox. In the early evenings the boys - mostly from a Boy's Camp down on Moon River - would have to pay a nickel a ticket to take a girl on the floor.

"They had many amateur nights and my girl friend dressed in a pale blue dress and sang, `Oh My Sweet Little Alice Blue Gown.' They also had costume evenings and we three girls won first prize one evening for dressing as hula dancers. We had picked our own straw (or hay or weeds) and made our own skirts. Years later we have gone there with our husbands to hear the big name bands for old times sake."

Leone's friend, Dorothy Smith Paget, writes with her own memories of those summers at Bala. "At least once a week I would go to Dunn's with Leone and Frances Palmer - we were in our very early teens. My mother and father loved to dance, especially when the band played the `Beer Barrel Polka.' One year - 1937 - we made Hawaiian costumes for the annual masquerade party and much to our surprise we came in first.

"After a few years we girls would go in on our own even though we sometimes had to walk the three miles from our cottage. It was worth the walk to dance at Dunn's; we usually got a ride home from boys we knew. Sometimes the boys from nearby Camp Pinecrest would walk home with us after the dance, with the promise of chocolate cake and a coke. This was a time when it was safe for young girls to be out alone. Our parents had no need to worry about us.

"Band concerts were held in the pavilion most Sunday nights and they brought in large crowds. I sang at these concerts at least once every summer. When my husband returned home near the end of WWII, we would paddle our canoe into Bala and drift outside the new pavilion, listening to the band playing. It seemed very romantic to us.

"The new pavilion was large and many more people could dance, but I don't think I will ever forget the fun we had in the old pavilion."

Original ice cream parlour chairs and table in Bala Museum.

THE ICE CREAM STORY

Did you know that:

Dunn's Pavilion sold more ice cream for Borden's every summer than any other outlet in Ontario -- or probably in Canada!

The Pavilion required two shifts of five waitresses to handle the demand on the giant soda fountain counter known as the Marine Bar.

Bala once had two competing ice cream parlours across town --
Langdon's (which Gerry Dunn bought in 1929)
and Carr's Ice Cream Parlour beside the falls.

Marshall Louch

Gerry may have been the CEO (Chief Entertainment Officer) of Dunn's Pavilion, but there were other individuals who were part of the team whose efforts combined to make this hall run as smooth as the still waters on the bay.

Writing about Dunn's would not be complete without bringing in Marshall Louch, who was as well known around the pavilion as Gerry himself. In fact, customers would sometimes confuse the two men, according to Marshall, who says people called him "Gerry" on more than one occasion. A reason for this confusion perhaps was the shifts they worked; when Marshall was supervising operations in the dancehall, Gerry would often be elsewhere, and vice versa.

I also interviewed Marshall Louch in the summer of 1994. Marshall was born in 1904, and at the age of 90 is only slightly younger than Gerry. The two are still great friends and keep in touch daily, usually via the telephone. While Gerry maintains his cottage on Acton Island, Marshall resides closer to town, living across from Bala in a cosy older home overlooking the falls. "With my binoculars I can even see who's going into the post office," he winks.

Born in London, Ontario, Marshall became involved in the performing end of the music industry, and actually played banjo with Guy Lombardo's first orchestra in 1919. Marshall's own band in 1918 was a Hawaiian style orchestra. At a very young age he travelled to Florida and performed in many of the famous, first-class hotels and ballrooms in places like Jacksonville and St. Augustine. He moved to this state and stayed for close to ten years. On one of his journeys from Canada to Florida, he and his young bride, Edith, boarded an ocean liner which caught fire at sea and listed dangerously to starboard. The couple lost everything, escaping in a lifeboat with only a blanket, but many other passengers were not so fortunate and perished in the tragic blaze.

Although he still travels to Florida with his daughter, Cathy Barber, and lives there for half the year, Marshall shakes his head when he speaks of the state. "I've seen it grow up and I've seen it deteriorate," he says, referring to the high crime rate in many of the cities.

"During the Depression I returned to Canada," says Marshall. "I was booked in with the Stanley St. John Band to the 21 Club in Port Carling, which was just opening in the mid-30's."

He ended up managing the club for five years, booking bands such as Jimmy Fry's orchestra. Saturday night was the big night of the week at the 21 Club, drawing upwards of 500 people. "A very good class of folks came to dance and enjoy themselves at Port Carling," says Marshall.

Located in the middle of the small town of Port Carling, the club's name was apparently coined from a nightclub in New York City. Inside, the 21 Club resembled a rustic cottage, with window awnings and split logs comprising the decor. Many people remember the 21 Club being jammed as people came by boat on the Muskoka Lakes, and by car. Some patrons would even make the long trip from Toronto for a night of fun in the

Artist Barbara Lepingwell's
depiction of dancers -
a gift from her to Marshall Louch

16

Top - 21 Club in Port Carling.
Centre - Sketch of interior.
Above - 1948 Photo of 21 Club's Staff.

town, travelling on poor roads and changing tires four or five times during the journey.

Through a mutual business interest in slot machines, Marshall became acquainted with Gerry Dunn who was expanding his operation in Bala.

Gerry eventually contacted Marshall to see if he might be interested in joining him at the pavilion. "It took me about two years to get together and seriously discuss the proposition with Gerry, but when I did it was agreed that I could try working there for one year initially," explains Marshall. The relationship transformed itself into a lengthy association for the two men. Marshall feels they were a good team for the business.

Gambling in Ontario?

Slot machines are not a recent source of amusement for the gambling public in Ontario. During the 1930's these Vegas-style one-arm bandits were as common as gum-ball machines in some parts of the province. Such as Bala.

An entrepreneur (who shall remain nameless in this book) had a circuit of locations throughout Muskoka where he had placed these slot machines, according to Marshall. Rumour had it that he distributed enough incentives to key people so that when a check was to be made by the police, he was given the word which he then passed on to his operators, including the 21 Club and Dunn's. As time passed, however, the government put down a firm foot on such enjoyment and the machines disappeared, for the time being.

Bruce Brocklebank remembers the days when Gerry Dunn had a few of these machines strategically placed in his store for customers to while away a few minutes as well as a few nickels. He writes: "I remember Gerry Dunn's first dancehall in 1938 or '40 or so. He had a dozen slot machines always on the go. Lots of American tourists and cottagers in those days. The slots were illegal by that time in Ontario, but not in Gerry's Drug Store - I remember him carrying a slot machine into his little office and take the back off and out would pour an ocean of nickels, and he even had 25-cent machines - too expensive for me. Anyway, that's how we figured he started up in a big way."

Ties For The Gents, Dresses For The Women

Dunn's resident photographer, Don McIndoe, says that everyone who went to Dunn's naturally liked Gerry, but also liked and respected Marshall. "Marshall was very visible and helped to maintain a high standard in the way the crowd dressed and how they behaved."

Marshall himself feels that in those days, the way people dressed affected their behaviour. "They always acted much better when they were dressed up. The hall was spic and span at all times, giving the patrons an atmosphere of class. Nobody wanted to really act up, and if they did, they would only embarrass themselves and their party."

Gerry Dunn also notes that a night out at his pavilion meant dressing up for the occasion. "We had a strict dress code, same as you would find in many of the Ontario dancehalls," he says. "Women wore dresses - often full-length - and men would wear shirt and tie. The only time of year when the dress code was relaxed was the final dance of the season at Thanksgiving. People at this dance would traditionally wear plaid shirts and casual pants. Part of the reason for the informality was that it was often cold at this time of year and there was no heat in the hall!" At this dance the people would join in with renditions of songs like `Good Night Ladies.' The store also closed up at this time.

"Gerry was the greatest person to work for," says Marshall. "If I had an idea I wanted to try, he gave me full permission to go ahead; if it worked, of course Gerry would be pleased, but if things did not turn out, Gerry never held it up to me."

Dunn's Pavilion was known to all musicians and their managers - even the big name entertainers - as one of the top venues to play, including when it came to receiving payment. Marshall explains: "With the U.S. acts, half the fee was sent when the booking was confirmed, and the remainder was paid the night of the job." One evening, as he gave Louis Armstrong's manager the cheque for the balance of his fees, Marshall said this man told him that Dunn's excellent reputation for payment was "known throughout the industry."

Marshall also remembers Tommy and Jimmy Dorsey's show at Bala. It was common knowledge that the two brothers did not get along with each other, but on stage they were complete professionals as they performed their great music for their fans. They even posed for Don McIndoe as he photographed them together on the Bala stage. "But they arrived and left in separate cars," says Marshall. "They wouldn't even speak to each other off stage."

Dunn's Runs Messages

In an era when communications were not instant, and the word "fax" might have been considered to be an improper spelling of the word "facts," people often telephoned the pavilion from far distances around the province and from parts of the U.S. They would leave messages for friends or family who were staying in the area, and Marshall Louch would then contact the local cabby to pick up the message and deliver it to the intended person. Marshall paid the cabby, and put the invoice in the till at the store. When the sender did arrive in Bala later in the summer, one of the first stops on their list was Dunn's, to pay for the service.

"We were the hub for Muskoka," says Marshall.

Dunn's eventually printed flyers to advertise the acts for the coming season, especially after so many people would telephone for this information.

One night Marshall took a telephone call from Bob Hope, calling for Les Brown who was playing at Dunn's that evening. "Les was able to leave the stage while the band was playing an instrumental to speak with Bob regarding a future engagement," says Marshall.

With such ties to Guy Lombardo and the city of London, it's small wonder that of all the bands to play Dunn's Pavilion, Marshall's all-time favourite was `Mr. Auld Lang Sang' himself, although the Lombardo brother he came to know best was Lebert. In fact, one of Marshall's most precious photographs was taken by Don McIndoe with Marshall and his wife Edith dancing in front of the stage with Guy Lombardo conducting his orchestra.

Time for a New Pavilion

As the 1930's drew to an end, the crowds became so large at the old pavilion that Gerry decided to tear down the hall and build what would become his famous pavilion, where all Muskoka would come to dance. He had visions of bringing the best bands in the business to Muskoka, but knew that he'd need a hall that could hold enough people to pay for the big acts.

"I designed the pavilion myself - no architect was involved," says Gerry. "It took some time on my part, coming up with different designs that I'd draw on the brown paper we used in the store to wrap things." Finally, with the help of local boat livery owner Mac Cunningham, the two men came up with a unique design for a hall with a 75-foot span that would be built out over the water. A structure of that width normally would require steel beams, but since this type of building material was in short supply due to the War, they had to use wood instead.

With a crew of 14 men, the pavilion began to take shape in late 1941. By utilising a gin pole (a high device for raising heavy weights) fashioned from a tall pine tree cut along the Moon River, they raised the upper rafters into place with Gerry at the top, nailing them down.

Next time you're in the pavilion, take a look up and picture a younger Gerry Dunn anchoring down those roof supports in 1941.

Inside the New Pavilion

The earliest picture of the new hall in 1942, before the fountain with coloured lights was installed, shows material hanging down from the ceiling. "These were natural cedar boughs dipped in calcium chloride for fire protection and then hung from the rafters for looks," says Gerry. The silver-coloured boughs served two functions - they camouflaged the wooden rafters which admittedly were a little unsightly, plus they helped improve the overall sound of the hall. Gerry says, "Bands always said they could play as loud as they liked and still sound good - there was no vibration."

The elegant interior of Dunn's Pavilion.
Top - cedar boughs camouflage the rafters.
Below - After the fountain was installed.

The hardwood dance floor was laid over thick tarpaper to prevent moisture from harming the maple wood. The tarpaper covered the main floor which was built on cement pylons. When the fountain was later installed in the centre of the dance floor, it became the focal point of the hall. The artificial potted palms and flowers throughout the hall, all blended together to enhance the atmosphere. Gerry says he got many of ideas for decorating from visiting dancehalls in the Detroit area when he was there during his early winters.

Even the stage was a conversation piece. It was raised about 18 inches from the floor, so dancers could be very close to the musicians. But it was the ambience created by the stage that blended in so well with the Muskoka environment. The backdrop of the bandstand was the facade of a small cottage with flower boxes underneath the windows, and palm trees and lamps adorning the platform.

There were a number of private boxes in the hall, each holding about 20 people. These partitions were popular when a group of individuals wanted to celebrate a special occasion.

Working at Dunn's

With the new pavilion and increasingly busy store, Gerry had to hire a sizeable staff. "We had a staff of about 35 working in the store and the pavilion," says Gerry. "This included the house band of eight members, booked for the summer, and a maintenance staff, servers, food and beverage staff for the hall, along with employees in the store. Almost everyone lived on the property for the summer." This gave Gerry the advantage of having his staff close at hand for their two shifts per day.

Cathy Barber, Marshall Louch's daughter, worked in Gerry's drug store at the pavilion for many years, and soon became one of the business' well known employees. She says that the staff and residents in the area were very much like a family. "People really cared for and about one another," she says. "Service was so personal in the store. For instance, young ladies would come in looking for just the right make-up to wear to the dance that evening, and the staff would help them make their decision. Patrons were welcomed back year after year, and if they had been ill, or hurt themselves the previous summer, genuine concern would be shown for their health. We kept track of our customers because we really cared about them," she says.

They also tried to keep track of staff members who worked there over the years, and where they have travelled in their lives. Girls were housed above the drug store and a strict curfew was imposed; boys lived over the ice house. Parents entrusted the management to watch over their kids for the summer, and knew that they were in good hands with Gerry and Marshall keeping a sharp eye on the staff. The supervision was there, but kids were also made to be responsible for their work habits and keeping their quarters clean. Still, every so often Marshall would throw out all the boys and do a full housecleaning himself.

Cathy says that working at Dunn's could make or break you. "You either shaped up, worked hard and generally grew and improved yourself, or you left. Most young people stood the test of Dunn's and stayed. Kids were not into drugs at this time, and if you drank, you would likely not be ready to show up for work first thing in the morning."

Being employed at Dunn's as a staff member during the summer and boarding on the premises in the facilities Gerry provided could be fun. Patricia Arney, who operates Balacade near the pavilion, remembers the summer of 1960 when she worked for Gerry and recalls experiences ranging from "living in an attic with 12 other girls sharing a gas station washroom and working four-hour shifts seven days a week, to almost running off with a drummer from Larry Elgart's band. My husband and I also have done business and been friends with all the subsequent pavilion owners."

Gerry says, "Two hotels in Bala were used by visiting bands from the U.S. while the house band stayed in quarters on the property." The house orchestra would often rehearse early in the day and play golf or take off up to Don McIndoe's cottage on the Moon River for some fun in the afternoon.

Meet
the
Staff

1942 - The First Summer

That first summer in the new pavilion in 1942 is memorable in many respects. James Gilmore remembers the thrill of the new dancehall. He writes: "Fifty years ago when I was courting my bride-to-be in Barrie, I was invited to the family cottage of Luke Spears on Lake Muskoka, five miles from Bala. Construction on the 'new' Dunn's Pavilion had been started in the fall of 1941 and when I arrived in Bala, there it was in all its splendour. Many a night we attended the dances, some of them the big bands, but more often to dance to the music of Howard Cable and his band and to hear his wonderful singer Norma Locke, who became Mart Kenney's wife.

"Mart Kenney also used to come on special occasions and we would try and attend the dances when he played. How wonderful to have Mart back in the summer of 1994 and be able to dance with him leading the band of Eddie Graf, who used to arrange music used by Mart Kenney in the old days."

Mart Kenney and Dunn's

In his autobiography, Mart Kenney reflects on his first visit to Dunn's. "On August 2, 1942, we drove north to Dunn's Pavilion at Bala....out over the water at the back of his drug store Gerry Dunn had built a pavilion with a good dance floor and seating for close to a thousand people....We played a midnight frolic from 12:01 a.m. to 3 a.m. Sunday night before the Monday Civic Holiday and the dance was such a success that we went back year after year on the closest Sunday to July 1, and the Sundays preceding Civic Holiday and Labour Day. It became a 'must' event. Gerry Dunn was held in great esteem by the hundreds who knew him, including old softie Gordon Sinclair, who was a fellow summer resident of Bala. Gerry was a very quiet-spoken, gentle person."

Leading up to the 1994 return engagement to Bala, Mart Kenney appeared on CBC radio to talk about some of his musical experiences. His orchestra did remote broadcasts wherever they performed, including Dunn's Pavilion. From an old CBC tape of the event, radio fans heard the introduction of the June 29, 1952, show as follows: "From beautiful Bala, Muskoka, CBC Dominion presents the Mart Kenney show......yes tonight from Dunn's Pavilion at Bala in the heart of the great Muskoka vacationland, the music of Canada's first man of showbusiness, Mart Kenney, some happy holiday talk between Maestro and friends, and some singing by the quartet, Four of a Kind - Wally Koster, Norma Locke, and Mart's guest tonight Chicho Viaje."

Mart's attentiveness to playing in perfect tune can be traced to 1934 when his orchestra did live broadcasts from the dance pavilion in Waterton Park, Alberta. The dancers here were Mormons who, according to Mart, "loved to dance to waltzes." Consequently, the band developed a style that was suitable for waltzes, with long musical notes which simply had to blend in perfect pitch. "Our sound was therefore excellent for broadcasting," says Mart. "We used muted brass and a lot of clarinets. We had been using clarinets for lead a long time before Glenn Miller did this."

It was indeed a special night in 1994 when Mart Kenney returned to Dunn's for a memorable evening of nostalgia, with Gerry Dunn the guest of honour. The evening was sponsored and MC'd by Jack Hutton. Jack also put together the 50th anniversary newspaper supplement Dunn's Pavilion in 1992. He and his wife run the Bala Museum and have a corner dedicated to Dunn's. A journalist by profession, Jack has worked for various newspapers, including the Telegram. He is also quite familiar with big bands, having played piano with the Rainbow Gardens Jazz Orchestra a number of years ago, and also as a student at Western.

Joan Stephenson and her husband Robert were just two of the hundreds of people in August, 1994, who dressed up and re-lived the more genteel days of the pavilion as they swayed across the floor to Mart's music. "It was fabulous," she writes. "A lot of bald and white-haired people dancin' up a storm."

Say "Cheese"

Since a night at Dunn's Pavilion was very special, it was only natural that people would want a souvenir or memento to remind them of the experience. A photograph was the ideal keepsake that would freeze the wonderful moment in time, so Gerry hired a resident `roving photographer' to circulate around the hall during the first portion of the evening, taking candid snaps of couples at the fountain, or groups of people at their tables. The idea wasn't unique - many of the swankier clubs in Ontario and throughout the U.S. offered this service to their customers - but it did mean that even today many people have a cardboard folder with `Souvenir of Dunn's Pavilion' printed on the front, and the five-by-seven black and white picture tucked safely inside. This promotion was also a money-maker for Gerry.

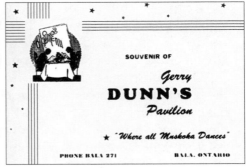

Resident photographers
Don and Winnifred McIndoe

Don McIndoe and his wife, Winnifred, took care of the photo duties at Dunn's Pavilion. The couple ran a photography business based in Hamilton, specializing in school photos and became involved with pavilion photography during the summer when the school picture side of their business finished in June.

Although they purchased their cottage on the Moon River 40 years ago and summered in Bala, Don also took his photography skills to the Club Aragon in Peterborough, the 21 Club in Port Carling, Paradise Gardens in Guelph, the Highlands in Galt, and many other venues where bands played and people danced, including Milford Manor and the Royal Muskoka Hotel.

"Our first year at Dunn's was 1948," says Don. "Each year we would start the first week of July." Their camera was called a Speedgraphic, a large instrument, similar to the big cameras used by professional newspaper photographers you often see in older movies.

"My wife would take pictures of couples throughout the evening while I worked feverishly in the darkroom developing prints," says Don. "The dark room was located just beside the women's washroom. Winnifred would deliver the photos in a souvenir folder before the dance finished. One night I went in to do some developing and there were women's dresses hanging on the wall. The Clooney sisters were using the dark room for changing when they performed that night," laughs Don. Usually, female singers would use the women's washroom which was located next door.

At the 21 Club in Port Carling Don's darkroom was located right beside the ice house. "I could set up anywhere - I just needed four walls with no light, or if necessary I'd block out any slivers of light that came in through the cracks."

Don would photograph the house bands at Dunn's, and also the big name orchestras and entertainers who played the hall. He has many informal and original photos of some of the biggest names in the music business, and often gave away these shots to patrons and people in the bands. "I took pictures of the orchestras posing before the crowd entered the hall and before the band actually started to play, because once the music began, the dance floor was filled," explains Don.

Don recalls one afternoon setting up his darkroom chemicals and hearing loud noises from the stage area. "That evening, Guy Lombardo was scheduled to perform and his band always used two grand pianos. Dunn's was equipped with one grand, but Marshall Louch had to track down another in the area and arranged to have it moved in that day, which was no small feat in the middle of the Muskoka area."

Very few negatives from the McIndoe's days remain today. "I destroyed the negatives at the end of the summer because they simply took up too much space," says Don. Fortunately, the couple does have many pictures in their personal collection, and were very kind to allow me to make copies.

With their cottage (which has since been sold) being located so close to the pavilion, Don and Winnifred became great friends with all the house bands. "Eddie Stroud, Ozzie Williams, Frank Evans - they all came over to our place to relax for an afternoon and for barbecues," says Winnifred. The couple's property featured 400 feet of shoreline with a beach, volleyball net and tennis court. Don also had a membership to a local golf club where his guests could play for free.

Below - Frank Evans led the house band at Dunn's Pavilion from 1956 -1963.

"Many of the house bands included music teachers or bandmasters as they were called," says Don. "It was a good way to make money, have a vacation and still keep your hand in music over the summer." But when the bands hopped on stage the vacation portion of the day was finished. "Bands would have to start precisely at 9:00 p.m. Gerry was insistent that the music start at that time, and not a minute late." At the end of each evening Marshall Louch would flick the lights indicating the dance was over. The lights would be turned up and the band would then play God Save the King (or Queen in later years) to finish the night.

Don echoes the words heard so frequently about Dunn's. "The crowds would line up long before the doors would open, and people came dressed up, regardless of their mode of transportation. Even those who arrived on expensive boats would be attired in good clothes, even though they might have to return on choppy water, or in the rain. Women wore dresses, often accented with a corsage, and men would arrive in jacket and tie." Dress codes were relaxed a little over the years, but people still wore good clothes for a night out at Dunn's.

Don talks about some of the entertainers he saw at Dunn's. "When a band like Les Brown played, musicians would arrive from everywhere, travelling great distances to watch and appreciate the fine talent in this band - never a bad note. Musicians also loved to watch Count Basie for the quality of professionalism he had on stage. Entertainers like Louis Armstrong and Duke Ellington were also great showmen. And the crowd would immediately respond to the Glen Miller Orchestra when they played tunes like `Moonlight Serenade' and `String of Pearls.'"

At the end of the season Don and Winnifred took group shots of the staff for that particular summer and would then make copies for each person. Many people who worked at Dunn's many years ago likely have their own picture stuffed away in a drawer or mounted in an album. Thanks to Don and Winnifred, much of Dunn's early history is chronicled pictorially.

Don retired from the business in the late 1970's and limits himself to personal photography today. The couple are also professional bridge instructors and take their skills on many ocean cruises around the world.

Dance and Romance

Cathy Barber remembers some of the many romances that developed at Dunn's. "Some girls on the staff would come in so excited about a new boy they had met, then in a couple of weeks it would have cooled off completely. And yet, some of these same couples got back together again and married."

The summer of 1954 was very special for 15-year-old Dinny Nimmo who vacationed on the Moon River in the cottage her grandfather built in 1920. Her first "real" date was going to the dance at Dunn's Pavilion and as she describes, the night was very special.

"The family at the beach had a boy from the city and he asked me to go dancing. It took a lot of talking and persuading for my grandmother to let me go, but it was a night I'll always remember. He didn't have a car, so he paddled me all the way to Bala. Walking into Dunn's was like stepping into a fantasy land. The shining dance floor, the tiers of little private tables, but best of all you could stand outside on the balcony and see the beautiful launches and canoes floating around listening to the same wonderful music from the big band.

"The next summer I actually had a boyfriend. When he invited me to go to Dunn's I was thrilled! I was a woman of experience, because I had been there before. I got all dressed up and he picked me up in the family car. It was an evening made for romance. Dancing at Dunn's never seemed to lose its magic.

"What is it that makes summer romances so special? Is it the sun-filled days and star-lit nights, or is it the innocence of it all?"

Donna and Ken Ketchen found a lot more than just a summer romance when Dunn's Pavilion brought them together. As parents and grandparents who have been married for many years, they can truly say it all began at Dunn's.

"I was 17 and just finished Grade 12 when I was hired by Gerry Dunn to work in his soda fountain for the summer of 1955 and what a summer it was for me," writes Donna. "It was the first time I had been away from home for any length of time and I went to Bala with much trepidation - entirely on my own.

"It was very hard work for little remuneration, but the people I met and the experiences I had made up for it. I certainly spent a lot of time dancing. The house band's trombone player was Laurie Bower. Tommy Dorsey was there that summer and the favourite song for me in 1955 was `Cherry Pink and Apple Blossom White.'

"However, the most memorable event that summer was meeting my future husband, Ken. He knew some of the girls who were working at Dunn's that summer and he and his friend came by to see if they would go to the dance that night. They were working but I wasn't so I went along; it seems so long ago. We were married in 1958 and we're still going strong. I have my picture from Dunn's Pavilion of all the staff and my `book of memories' - where everyone wrote something about that summer."

Now here is Ken's recollection of 1955:

"As a young fellow growing up in the '50's in the town of Port Credit, I always looked forward to heading north for the weekend. One summer home our family rented year after year was on the Moon River in Bala. At that time Bala was a bustling summer community with Dunn's Pavilion being the centre of attraction for a lot of people. Dunn's not only had a soda counter, but a drug store section that sold a wide variety of goods. Needless to say, the large dancehall at the back was extremely popular bringing in all those top name dance bands.

"As I progressed through my teens I felt a real urge and need to partake of this beautiful romantic place overlooking Lake Muskoka. I can remember finally getting up enough nerve to ask a young lady to accompany me to the dance, only to find she was in Bala without a dress. Well, that didn't stop me - I went home and asked my mother if she might have a dress that would fit. That didn't work out either, so we had to be satisfied sitting around the pavilion outside, listening to the music and wishing we were there.

"One weekend in the early part of the summer of 1955 a good friend and I were looking for a date for the Saturday night dance. This particular summer there were a few female students from Port Credit High School working behind the counter at Dunn's. Unfortunately, the majority of the PCHS girls would be working that night but they said that the girls not working might be interested. Well, we made our appearance at the appointed time later that afternoon. I don't recall how the conversation went, but these two girls did agree to join us that evening.

"As soon as my friend and I left the late afternoon appraisal, we began discussing who would have the blonde from Port Credit or the brunette from Milton. Since he preferred blondes and I was partial to brunettes, no argument ensued. We didn't stop to think where their preferences might lie.

"We had a great evening tripping over each other on the

dance floor, having our pictures taken by the roving photographer and strolling along the dock and balcony under the beautiful Muskoka sky.

"Although I did not see this young lady in Bala again that summer, I did invite her to attend the C.N.E. with me the following Labour Day weekend. Over the next three years we would see each other about once a week, taking in such places as the Brant Inn in Burlington, Leisure Lodge, etc, and finally in 1958 we were married. Close to 40 years later we are the proud parents of three great children and grandparents to one."

Joan Olesuk writes: "My best memories and fun times were in Muskoka; I worked at Bala Manor, New Windsor Hotel and Muskoka Beach Inn (now Muskoka Sands). It seemed like we went dancing almost every night between Bala and Torrance. Dunn's Pavilion was my favourite - Gerry Dunn was a great man. I danced to most of the big bands, and still enjoy dancing. I have an autographed record album that I won in Bala coming second in a jitterbug contest."

Complimentary Pass signed by Marshall Louch

When Louis Armstrong Played

Louis Armstrong's appearance at Dunn's in 1962 is still remembered by many fans as quite possibly the most memorable night in the pavilion's history. It was one of those rare occasions when all the elements necessary for the creation of a magical night of music somehow came together, as if Gerry knew his days at the hall were coming to an end, and he wanted to give his customers one very special evening they would never forget. The sky glimmered with a million stars, the evening air was warm and gentle, the water of Lake Muskoka was calm, mirroring the overhead celestial body's canopy as well as the welcoming lights of the pavilion and surrounding cottages.

Over 2100 people heeded the urge to make their pilgrimage

to Dunn's to see one the greatest jazzmen of their time perform. Another estimated 1,000 people lolled on the grass outside, or quietly drifted around the bay in every imaginable type of vessel, from canoes to gleaming varnished wooden watercraft appointed with polished brass fixtures, enjoying Louis Armstrong's music as it wafted from the pavilion's open windows into the soft night air.

Gerry Dunn still remembers that night. "Louis Armstrong drew the largest crowd ever - over 2100," says Gerry. "It was 1962 and that night we sold over $5,000 in mix and ice alone. We charged five dollars admission, the most we'd ever charged to that point."

Thirty-five years later, people who were there still talk about this magnificent event. My former music teacher and his wife, Ben and Lil Rose, were part of this slice of Bala's history. They came by boat and savoured the moment from the water.

John Bennie writes that he spent many evenings at the Brant Inn in Burlington and at Dunn's in Bala. "I remember one summer evening having dinner with my date in a small restaurant in Bala prior to a Louis Armstrong dance at Dunn's. It wasn't a fancy place. Louis Armstrong and his wife came into the restaurant quietly and sat down at the next table to have dinner. No fuss was made even though there were others in the room; they talked quietly. Would this have been possible in the U.S.A. at that time? I think not."

Probably the most touching letter I have received for this book comes from Mrs. D. Castaldi, who wrote about her memorable experience the night that Louis Armstrong played at Dunn's Pavilion:

"My aunt and uncle had a cottage just down the lake from Bala Bay. It was the family centre every summer from the time I was a very small child till I was at least in my late teens. As youngsters, my cousins and I used to go into Dunn's and wander through the store with our little bit of spending money deciding from all the exciting things we found there, what we would buy. Then the day came when we became big enough to go with our families to the dance upstairs. What a great room it was with its sunken dance floor and tables all around. We sure felt like big girls.

The great Louis Armstrong provided
many fond memories for his fans.

"One evening when we were there for the dance to listen to Louis Armstrong and his band, my father asked me to dance. I'm sure I was probably the youngest person there. Boy, did I think I was grown up and special. And what happened next has stayed with me my entire life. Louis was singing, and when an instrumental break came, he stepped down from the bandstand and asked me: `May I have this dance with you?' You could imagine the thrill that this was for me, and for my parents too. This memory has been one of my fondest all my life, and I never hear Louis' music that I don't remember this special moment.

"As we grew older, sometimes the whole family would pile into the boat and go up to the water under the pavilion, anchor and just sit and enjoy the music from the bands floating across the water in Bala harbour.

"And of course as we got to the dating age, many an evening was spent in the boat with your `special guy,' anchored near the pavilion feeling very romantic with the full moon and great music. And once in a while, when money allowed, we even got the chance to put on our summer finest and go into the hall and dance the night away in the arms of your current sweetie. It was wonderful, you could actually dance to the music and talk without loud music drowning your words. You could always hear those sweet nothings whispered in your ear."

Gerry Dunn
Presents
PARADE OF BANDS
For Coming Season

Sat. June 29	**OFFICIAL OPENING**	With FRANK EVANS and his Orchestra (Dancing every week-night during July and August)
Sun. June 30	**SUNDAY MIDNITE DANCE**	
Tues. July 16	**GLEN MILLER Orchestra**	under the direction of RAY McKINLEY
Tues. July 23	**LOUIS ARMSTRONG**	SATCHMO and his ALL STARS
Tues. July 30	**WOODY HERMAN**	and his AWARD WINNING ORCHESTRA
Sun. Aug. 4	**SUNDAY MIDNITE DANCE**	
Tues. Aug. 6	**LES ELGART**	and his FAMOUS ORCHESTRA
Tues. Aug. 13	**JIMMY DORSEY BAND**	STARRING "LEE CASTLE" as conductor
Sun. Sept. 1	**SUNDAY MIDNITE DANCE**	
Sat. Oct. 12	**THANKSGIVING PARTY**	Muskoka's most colourful Fall attraction

TUESDAY
AUG. 16
Les
BROWN
AND HIS
BAND of RENOWN
DUNN'S
PAVILION • BALA
ADMISSION $2.50 per PERSON

Gerry Dunn's Pavilion
BALA
"WHERE ALL MUSKOKA DANCES"

Special Coming Events

Wednesday, July 1st	**KING GANAM and His Orchestra** Square and Round Dancing	Admission $2.00 each
Saturday, July 4th	**OFFICIAL OPENING** FRANK EVANS and his ORCHESTRA (Dancing every week-night during July & August)	
Thursday, July 16th	**LOUIS ARMSTRONG** and his ORCHESTRA	Admission $3.00 each
Tuesday, July 21st	**LES BROWN** and his BAND of RENOWN	Admission $2.50 each
Wednesday, July 29th	**LARRY ELGARD** and his ORCHESTRA	Admission $2.50 each
Sunday, August 2nd	**CIVIC HOLIDAY MIDNIGHT DANCE** FRANK EVANS and his ORCHESTRA	Admission $2.00 each
Wednesday, August 5th	**THE TOMMY DORSEY ORCHESTRA** Directed by WARREN COVINGTON	Admission $2.50 each
Wednesday, August 12th	**DUKE ELLINGTON** and his ORCHESTRA	Admission $2.50 each
Tuesday, August 18th	**THE GLENN MILLER ORCHESTRA** with RAY McKINLEY	Admission $2.50 each
Sunday, September 6th	**LABOR DAY MIDNIGHT DANCE** FRANK EVANS and his ORCHESTRA	Admission $2.50 each
Saturday, October 10th	**THE THANKSGIVING PARTY** Square and Round Dancing	Admission $2.00 each

Les Brown and His Band of Renown
attracted both dancers and musicians.

Left - drummer Shelly Mann

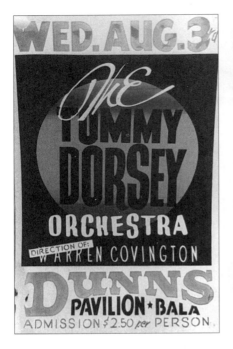

Performers at Dunn's included international stars such as Warren Covington, Stan Kenton and Jewel Brown.

Top - Les Elgart and his Orchestra.

Count Basie and Duke Ellington were the superstars of their day.

DUNNS PAVILION ★ BALA

For your DANCING PLEASURE!

Guy Lombardo

AND HIS ROYAL CANADIANS

MON. JUNE 30

ADMISSION $5.00 PER PERSON

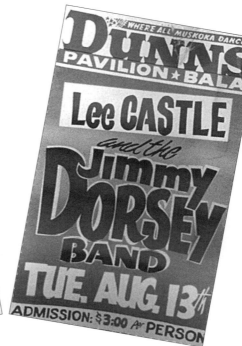

WHERE ALL MUSKOKA DANCES...

DUNNS PAVILION ★ BALA

Lee CASTLE and the Jimmy DORSEY BAND

TUE. AUG. 13th

ADMISSION: $3.00 Per PERSON

WHERE ALL MUSKOKA DANCES

DUNNS PAVILION ★ BALA

TEEN DANCING EVERY FRIDAY

AUG 6	The COUNTDOWNS
AUG 13	The BIG TOWN BOYS
AUG 20	The REGENTS with DUNC & JUDI
AUG 27	JEOFF AND THE CONTINENTALS
SEPT 3	JON & LEE AND THE CHECKMATES

ADMISSION: $1.25 per PERSON

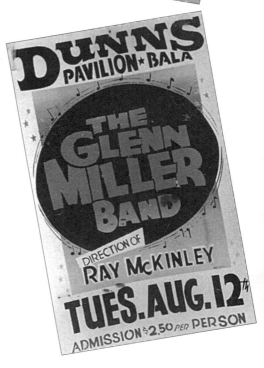

DUNNS PAVILION ★ BALA

THE GLENN MILLER BAND

DIRECTION OF RAY McKINLEY

TUES. AUG. 12th

ADMISSION $2.50 PER PERSON

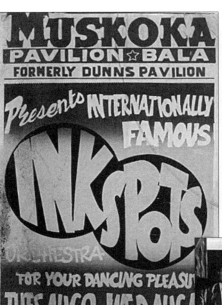

MUSKOKA
PAVILION ☆ BALA
FORMERLY DUNNS PAVILION
Presents INTERNATIONALLY
FAMOUS
INK SPOTS
ORCHESTRA
FOR YOUR DANCING PLEASURE
TUES AUG 9 WED AUG 1
ADMISSION 2.50 per PERS

WHERE ALL MUSKOKA DANCES...
DUNNS
PAVILION ☆ BALA
TUESDAY
JULY 30th
WOODY
Herman
and his ORCHESTRA
ADMISSION: $3.00 Per PERSON

Posters (now collectors' items) advertised coming attractions such as the Ink Spots.

Count Basie makes another appearance.

Pee Wee Hunt and Richard Maltby's Orchestras.

The Little Dancehall in Torrance

It would be appropriate at this point to pause for a moment and take a peek at a small dance pavilion, located just a couple of miles south of Dunn's, in the hamlet of Torrance. If Dunn's Pavilion represented everything that was formal and grand during the Big Band years, this small dancehall down the road stood in stark contrast, providing just the cosy informal atmosphere lots of kids wanted to take in after an evening at Bala. It wasn't unusual for young staff members from Dunn's to make the short trek down to Torrance after the dance for a campfire on the beach and a dance in the little pavilion.

Rita Frederickson lives across the street from the lot and remembers this hall quite well. "Jim Kidd built the pavilion in the late 1930's," she says. "He also ran a small store in the community. The street on which it was located was later named Queen's Walk after Queen Elizabeth stepped out of an automobile, walked a few steps to the train station and hopped aboard a train during a 1959 royal visit.

"My sister Eileen and her husband Bert purchased the pavilion after World War II. They ran Saturday night dances with the music supplied by the jukebox. There were never any live bands but it was a popular spot for local kids to dance." Rita and her husband John would often work at the pavilion.

George Allison, whom we met earlier, spent most of his summers as a youth and then as a young man in Bala, dancing to the famous Big Bands. As much as this experience is still vivid, he still has a special place in his heart for Torrance and writes: "I think my favourite pavilion, when I really look back, was the little pavilion at Torrance by the dock. It had no more than a 12 by 15 foot dance floor, smoothly sanded and quite springy, with only a 2" by 6" railing that was uncomfortable to sit on, which made everybody dance - even the boys who were just emerging from the `I hate girls' stage. It was an early teen place with a jukebox that played the right stuff and had absolutely no attraction for adults. What a plus! They sold ice cream and pop and played a freebie on the jukebox every fifth or sixth piece. How good could it get?"

Rita explains what eventually happened to this unique little hall. "The actual pavilion in Torrance collapsed a number of years ago under the weight of winter snow. It had not been used as a dancehall for many years; after the collapse the debris was removed, the land was cleared and eventually a home was erected on the site."

Economics of the time did not allow everyone the luxury of dressing up in good clothes and taking in a dance at Dunn's says Rita. "But if you just wanted an evening of fun, many cottagers and residents from Torrance would canoe up to Bala and drift outside the pavilion just to listen to the music."

Time to Move On, Says Gerry

Yes, both Dunn's and Bala have changed over three decades, though the transition has been gradual. By 1963 Gerry was entertaining thoughts of selling the pavilion. It came as a surprise to many people who assumed that both Gerry and his dancehall would go on indefinitely, but the time had come to move on. Gerry was becoming increasingly frustrated from the clamp-down on the pavilion's BYOB policy. Jack Hutton feels that one of the contributing reasons to Gerry's decision was due to this increased pressure and hassle from the authorities. People were also starting to bring in more than a mickie and society was becoming aware of the fact that drinking too much at a dance and then driving wasn't such a good idea.

The Big Band era was also beginning to wane. And as Jack says, "It was also becoming more expensive for large orchestras to travel and pay members."

Dancehall operators sometimes smile and shake their heads when they hear people talking about the "gold mine" it is assumed they must have on their hands. Providing entertainment for people is much more demanding than one might realize. The dance business is one of the few types of operations where you have to safely welcome anywhere from 300 to over 1,000 people into your establishment in less than one hour, give them an evening of pleasure, ensure that no trouble erupts, monitor the crowd's behaviour for potential problems, provide your patrons with food and refreshment, oversee your staff, deal with the band, comply with all the applicable regulations and laws governing such a business, be prepared for unforseen emergencies, and finally ensure that people leave the premises in an orderly fashion and hope they'll return to the next dance.

There are many more tasks involved than simply turning the key to open a store and clicking on the cash register. The dance business takes a very special type of person who is able to combine warm hospitality with shrewd business sense in order to successfully manage a dancehall.

Was Dunn's Pavilion a gold mine? Well, just like the Klondike gold rush, most of the riches discovered were earned through hard work. And perhaps a bit of luck.

So it was with dance pavilions. Gerry Dunn at no time in his career sat back and simply assumed business would come his way. He worked at his enterprise just as hard as any other successful entrepreneur does, managing his staff, directing maintenance and renovation projects, carefully purchasing saleable items for his store, providing a popular meeting place at his soda fountain, greeting people and shaking their hands at his dances......in short, he was a hands-on proprietor, a people person, a warm and likeable individual who gave the people what they wanted at the time. He also had to anticipate the dance band entertainment and retail products that would please his pavilion and store customers in the future. Gerry never had time to put up his feet and count his "gold."

Pat Dunn, Les Elgart, Gerry Dunn, Eddie Stroud, Larry Elgart

47

Downhill in the Mid-60's

The subsequent owner, unfortunately, was not as astute as Gerry Dunn, according to observers. After Gerry sold the business in 1963, Marshall Louch stayed with the next operator, but says this person would not listen to the advice that he offered. Poor management, combined with the inability to accept the fact that the Big Band era was winding down as rock 'n' roll rose in popularity, resulted in the owner losing the pavilion to the bank a few years later.

The advent of rock music marked a turning point in the future success of dance pavilions in general. Jerry Lee Lewis, Roy Orbison, Carl Perkins and even Johnny Cash were all starting their careers in the mid-1950's. As well, artists like Bill Haley and the Comets, Bobby Darin, Pat Boone, Buddy Holly and the Crickets, Richie Valens and many others were all becoming the new teen idols. Black artists including Chuck Berry, Fats Domino and Little Richard were also enjoying fame as hot new stars of the 1950's.

Yes, rock 'n' roll was here to stay.

And the King of Rock, the man who is really credited with heading this tidal wave of new music that swept the continent and indeed the western world with a surge that had never before been experienced was of course, Elvis Presley. Then The Beatles arrived, spear-heading the musical British invasion, and shortly thereafter came the new generation of American and Canadian rock groups of the 1960's.

The owners and operators of dance pavilions around Ontario who could anticipate, or at least realize, that change was part of their business, were able to make this transition into the era of rock 'n' roll music; as a result, they enjoyed a number of prosperous years catering to a new generation of young people. The Baby Boomers were entering their teens and wanted to go dancing, just like their parents, but these kids wanted to move to a different tune.

Luria Catsell, a San Francisco political activist, said in 1965, "Rock 'n' roll is the new form of communication for our generation.....music is the most beautiful way to communicate, it's the way we're going to change things. Half the population is teenaged now.....Dancing is the thing."

Author Ralph Gleason wrote, "Dancing reflected the general attitude of self-expression.....The actual demand for dances is going to increase. The whole rock revolution points to dancing, the music ineluctably moves one to move.....It is harmless and it is legal. It is, in fact, a delight."

When Ray Cockburn entered the Bala picture in 1968, the pavilion Gerry Dunn had built in 1942, and carefully nurtured into one of the most successful dancehalls of its type in Canada, had declined into a sorry state of financial woes and physical disrepair.

And Up Again With Ray Cockburn at the Helm

Purchasing the pavilion in Bala was not particularly risky for Ray after 10 years under his belt as owner of the immensely popular Pavalon (known as The Pav) on Lake Couchiching in Orillia.

When Gerry Dunn's years at the hall finished in 1963, the following owner did not seem to have the knack for the business and perhaps was not aware of the work required to run a successful hall. Ray agrees with Marshall's observations that this person loved the Big Bands and did not wish to move into rock 'n' roll, even though the market was changing and kids wanted to dance and listen to this new music. In any case, the bank was forced to repossess the pavilion and soon approached Ray Cockburn to see if he was interested in acquiring a second venue, since he was very successful in Orillia with The Pav.

"I agreed, and was able to purchase the hall for a very reasonable amount," says Ray. "The bank even foot the bill to tear down the existing store in front of the building - it had been condemned and had to be demolished." Ray then built the extension on the front of the Bala pavilion.

By the mid-60's the name of the pavilion became rather confusing to people. It seemed to waffle between Dunn's Pavilion and Muskoka Pavilion, as seen on some of the posters which remain today. The label "Kee" came about as a solution to remove the uncertainty in customers' minds regarding the hall's name.

Ray says that he did a lot of advertising, especially by the use of posters which he hung himself throughout cottage country.

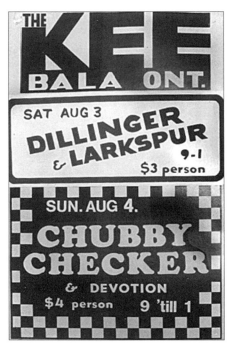

THE KEE
BALA ONT.

SAT AUG 3
DILLINGER
& LARKSPUR
9-1
$3 person

SUN. AUG 4.
CHUBBY
CHECKER
& DEVOTION
$4 person   9 'till 1

"A short name, easily remembered, was what I wanted, and when someone suggested that the pavilion was the `key' to Bala and the surrounding Muskoka area, I jumped at the idea and changed the spelling to KEE." There was some period of adjustment when people would telephone the hall, expecting to hear Dunn's Pavilion, and be greeted with The Kee, but the new name has held since 1968.

The largest crowd at The Kee was the night The Stitch in Tyme and Lighthouse played, drawing 2300, 200 more than attended the Louis Armstrong dance in 1961. Another night saw 2250 cram into the hall. There was standing room only and all chairs were removed except the benches which were attached to the floor.

It was Ray's idea to book two bands per night into The Kee. The sound system was old, which resulted in a poor reproduction for recorded music. "By having two bands on stage, live music was continuous, leaving little time for kids to become distracted," Ray explains. The first band was usually a very well-known act, with the second band playing for the exposure that the Bala stage would bring. Also, by giving bands one night at The Pav in Orillia and another at The Kee, Ray could obtain a more reasonable rate for the group.

The famous cedar boughs strung from the rafters at Dunn's were taken down after one of the bands ruined a few while stringing up electrical cords. After these boughs fell, it was decided to remove all of them. Interestingly, these boughs which Gerry had treated in calcium chloride many years ago, were still fire-proof. "We tried to light one with a match and it simply would not take a flame," says Ray.

Thoughts from the Late '60's

A couple of years after Joanne Farrell danced at Greenhurst Pavilion on Sturgeon Lake in the 1960's, she discovered The Kee to Bala and writes with her memories: "The music with Major Hooples Boarding House, Mandala's rendition of `White Rabbit', Motherlode, Coney Hatch and a summer romance with a guy I met from Bracebridge. His name was Carl and boy, could he dance. We were high on life and love that summer. I remember the `heat' in the Kee around 11 p.m. when the wooden dance floor literally shook and bounced. The place would be filled to capacity and body to body - everyone grooved to the tunes. I loved it all!

"I feel sorry that my 18-year-old daughter may never experience how truly special it is to dance in a pavilion on a lake up North in cottage country. Those treasured, innocent memories will stay with me forever."

In 1971 Ray was approached by the Parry family who indicated they were interested in purchasing the pavilion. "It was rather spur-of-the-moment, but I did agree to sell," says Ray.

The Kee, The Parrys and the 1970's

Bev Parry and her family had many successful years at the Kee, taking the pavilion through the 1970's and into the next decade. With music being an art form that never sits still, the Parrys had to move with the various phases of rock 'n' roll.

The price of bands was still fairly reasonable for a few years, but as this cost of doing business rose, so did the price they had to charge at the door. It became obvious that for the Kee to remain viable and compete with bars and other forms of entertainment available to people, a liquor license had to be obtained, so they set the wheels in motion. The Kee has now had a license for close to 25 years.

A very young Adam Parry (Bev's son) was learning the dance pavilion business during this time. He swept floors,

THE **KEE**
BALA MUSKOKA CANADA

HOLIDAY
WEEK - END

•• 4 HOURS OF CONTINUOUS MUSIC ••
FRIDAY JULY 1 — FEATURING

HARBINGER
9:00 P.M. $3.☎ per person

SATURDAY JULY 2 — FEATURING

IAN THOMAS
& HIS BAND
9:00 P.M. $3.75 per person

FRI. JULY 8 - DACKER'S CAT
SAT. JULY 9 - SWEET BLINDNESS

Top - The Kee today still features the tables and chairs installed by Gerry.

Above - View from the stage shows the upper balcony.

Left - The original stage with the backdrop of a cottage facade is now the bar.

sold admission tickets, cooked food, learned how to hire entertainment and generally acquired the wide range of experience necessary to successfully manage a hall. He and his wife Andrea (who hails from Bala) later went on to purchase Greenhurst Pavilion on Sturgeon Lake.

Joe Kondyjowski's Years

Joe is one of the most successful dance pavilion operators in the province, having owned or managed four major venues in Ontario, including Greenhurst Pavilion, Oshawa's Jubilee Pavilion, The Kee to Bala, and his current hall, The Red Barn Auditorium in Oshawa.

Joe is a man of action, a man who, when he eyes a job that should be done, simply takes charge and sees the project through to its completion. As a person who loves to preserve the original integrity of older buildings, taking over the Kee in the 1980's presented a number of challenges for Joe. The pavilion Gerry Dunn had built was well out over the water, and much of the structure sat on cribbing and pylons that had been installed in 1942. As Joe says, "We had much work to do!"

And work he did. Fortunately for Joe, with his experience and sound management, the pavilion brought in great rock 'n' roll acts and consequently large crowds. In other words, there was sufficient revenue to support the huge expense that Joe incurred in bringing this marvellous old building up to the standards necessary to keep it operating.

"I owned The Kee for six years and in that time I did more work on it than any previous owner after Gerry Dunn," says Joe. "I had a new Viceroy home built on the property. We poured asphalt for a parking area, installed a new roof and built a new deck." Warm summer nights on Dunn's deck is an experience recalled by many people, but the old one was simply falling apart. Joe also brought back the Big Bands three times per season during his stay, the first owner to do so in many years.

"We had to also put in new cement cribs, and very slowly, in stages we jacked up the building because it had begun to sink. The pilings underneath were all replaced. A new kitchen was put into the building and we painted the outside. I wanted to create a Cape Cod type of feel, so we went for a whitish blue/grey tone with slate blue trim."

The most special moment for Joe arrived when Gerry Dunn stopped by the pavilion. Although Joe often saw Gerry drive by in his boat, he had never made a request to come in. After the paint job, Joe made a point of inviting Gerry to stop by, take a tour and have a look at the building he had erected nearly fifty years ago.

Says Joe, "Gerry said he was very pleased and commented `the place had not looked this good since I sold it in 1963.' That was the ultimate compliment for me."

Joe was the first operator of The Kee to start booking big name rock acts. His first experience was with Burton Cummings, and Burton has returned to the Kee almost every year since. "Burton is a consummate professional who puts on a first-rate show for his fans. He was great to get along with - one night he even took requests from the crowd for over an hour. They loved it. Burton also started a tradition of writing creative verses on the band's dressing room wall, a custom that was followed by many other bands."

In the late 1980's Joe sold the business to Norman Arbour, who had also operated the Highlands in Galt, a popular pavilion in that area of Ontario. Arbour apparently had a tough time with the LCBO, and after a year decided to move to Florida, where at last word he owns a couple of liquor stores, says Joe. Sanober Patel then purchased the business and assumed responsibilities as owner. Since Sanober was relatively new to the business, Joe returned to Bala and spent one full summer helping her with various aspects of managing the pavilion, imparting some of the advice and techniques which had been passed on to him by veteran pavilion owners such as Mrs. Lines at Greenhurst and Owen McCrohan at Oshawa's Jubilee Pavilion.

Sanober Patel

Sanober acquired the Kee in 1990 and was ably assisted in the business by her son, Jim. The pavilion was continuing its tradition as a summer dancehall, opening in May and closing on the Thanksgiving weekend. The hall is not heated - in fact the water must be turned off by Thanksgiving to prevent pipes from freezing. During the months of operation Sanober and Jim experienced the realities that all previous owners faced - running a successful business at The Kee involved working 16-hour days, seven days a week.

"Providing entertainment for the area is a constant challenge," says Sanober in our 1994 interview. "We bring in top name rock acts and must pay them top dollar for their services." As a result, the admission customers pay at the door is fairly high, ranging anywhere from $8 to $25 per person, depending on the band being presented on a particular night. However, when you compare this to the five dollar admission people paid to see Louis Armstrong, and factor in inflation, the price is not unreasonable. Sanober says, "In this business, gate receipts usually cover the band's fee, while the bar and concession stand cover operating costs and hopefully, some profit." Gone are the days when 2100 people could cram into the hall; it's licensed for about 700 today.

When I visited with Sanober in 1994 she was expanding the horizons of The Kee by introducing a variety of entertainment on mid-week nights, such as Yuk-Yuk's comedy on Thursdays during the summer. Also, a new attraction called the Resort Olympics was being tried out that year. People in the area were bussed in by staff members for an evening of fun and games. Although attendance could have been better, the first night was a great success judging by people's comments, and they promised to return with their friends for future Resort Olympic nights. Sanober donated the use of the Kee during the fall Cranberry Festival for the display of art.

The Kee is now 95% rock and roll, according to Sanober. She schedules one night of country and western and one night of Big Band music each season, mainly to recognize the Kee's history, which originated with the Big Band sound. The older members of the community also appreciate these nights. The fact is,

In 1992, writer, businessman and musician, Jack Hutton, wrote a special newspaper supplement to honour the 50th anniversary of Dunn's Pavilion. Jack also runs the Bala Museum.

country music and dance band music simply do not bring out the numbers of people that rock draws. And as other operators have pointed out, the older audiences come out to dance to the music, and make fewer trips to the bar.

"Our customers come from everywhere - from local towns such as Bracebridge, Gravenhurst and Orillia to further away centres like Toronto and Buffalo," says Sanober. With the exception of the Dardanella at Wasaga Beach, there is virtually no other dance pavilion with the capacity and the atmosphere of the Kee which still operates on a regular basis.

After Sanober's arrival she had the complete exterior of the building painted, changing the colour from Joe's Cape Cod bluish-white, to a light green tone. She has also provided an in-house P.A. system for entertainers, which she rents for the season. These huge speakers are set up to provide the best sound for the hall, and all bands playing here use the system, complete with sound mixing board. Usually, rock bands carry their own P.A., so using the Kee's equipment eliminates a major task for bands when they set up their equipment - all they need to bring with them is their own stage gear. An extensive lighting system has also been installed in the wooden rafters that Gerry Dunn once lifted with a gin pole and assembled himself, over 50 years ago.

The stage was originally located in front of the cottage facade. Sanober gives us some background on the changes made here. "During the late 1970's a new stage was built, on the east side of the dance floor, at least twice the size of the old platform and much higher - it is about four or five feet high." The old cottage front has been left standing, but instead of potted palm trees and flower boxes underneath the windows, a bar has been installed.

The familiar fountain which was once located in the middle of the dance floor, illuminated by coloured lights and surrounded with green boughs is just a memory. All that remains of this elegant prop are two small pieces of sheet metal covering holes on the dance floor, indicating the former sources of water and electricity for the fountain.

Stephen Wyllie

During the summer of 1994 Sanober was approached by concert promoter and entrepreneur Stephen Wyllie, who asked her if she would be interested in selling the business. As is the case with many aspects of life, Steve's inquiry just happen to come at the right time - Sanober decided to turn over the pavilion's operation to the new owner.

The transition began in 1995, with Steve assuming full ownership of the property in 1996.

Every new operator of The Kee to Bala has brought his or her plans, hopes and dreams for the pavilion. They realize that it is not simply another concert hall or dancehall; there is so much history behind Dunn's Pavilion that ownership also brings with it a responsibility to the residents, cottagers and visitors to Muskoka who regard the pavilion as one of the most familiar and significant landmarks in the region.

Steve has a deep awareness of the importance that The Kee holds for so many people. "Practically every day someone will stop by, knock at the pavilion door and talk about the good times they had dancing here," he says.

And Steve has already set the wheels in motion to honour the rich past of his pavilion. Re-painting the pavilion to its original Muskoka white with green trim was Steve's first job on his long list of "to-do's." Three Big Band dances were scheduled for the 1996 summer, and to bring back the memories for this age group Steve brought in carpenters to adjust the original stage area to accommodate the orchestra. "The white picket railing in front of the bar can now be removed, the bar is covered with the scrim (curtain) from the big stage, and for the first time in nearly 20 years the orchestra now performs on the original stage," explains Steve. For these special dances, tables and chairs are installed on the high stage used for rock shows, and a temporary railing is set up along the edge of this platform. Steve even had a large sign painted to hang behind the band: "Dunn's Pavilion, Established 1942." Future plans include installing a new coloured fountain in the centre of the dance floor where so many people remember posing for a McIndoe photograph.

For many years a small but interesting building has sat beside The Kee, and has often been referred to simply as The

Garage. With its double sharp-peaked gables, the structure resembles a small non-descript cottage, but this dwelling has served a number of purposes. Built well over six decades ago, it was first used by Gerry Dunn as a gas and service station. People could fill up, have their oil checked, purchase automotive supplies and have minor repairs done. When the gas station business was discontinued, it was a natural decision to use the building to house some of the staff who worked at Dunn's. Subsequent owners have utilized the old gas station as accommodation for bands, and in recent years for storage of various material related to the dancehall. Stephen is currently renovating The Garage and is planning to resurrect this structure in 1997 under the name Dunn's Station, an ice cream parlour and souvenir shop.

Gerry's old gas station is being converted into Dunn's Station.

"My plans also include promoting this location as a Muskoka historical site which hopefully would be included on boat tours of the lake, such as the Segwun," says Steve. He feels the hall would make an ideal location where people could stop by during the day, tour the pavilion and perhaps see a film documenting the wonderful years the hall has seen. Another idea Steve is considering is staging a mid-week jazz night on the terrace. "I don't think anyone would mind hearing some fine evening music wafting over the water," says Steve. "The pavilion has apparently never had a complaint about the music being too loud."

They shouldn't - Dunn's Pavilion has been there longer than most people have.

Whether you swayed to the Big Bands at Dunn's Pavilion (above), or cheered your favourite rock act at The Kee (below), the magic of this pavilion spans many generations.

Meanwhile, today's bills have to be paid and that means The Kee must continue as a viable attraction for music fans. Steve lives, sleeps and breathes his business from early April to late October, travelling thousands of miles during the season in his trusty blue 1974 Volkswagen Bug, plastering posters and promoting his shows from Huntsville to Barrie and beyond. When he's finished his advertising chores he's talking to agents, booking bands, overseeing the continual maintenance and repairs the hall requires, and greeting people seeking tickets for upcoming shows. Oh, and there's always the regular stream of folks who stop by to reminisce a little.

Owner Stephen Wyllie pays tribute to his pavilion's history.

"At our first Big Band dance for 1996 I spoke with a couple who had originally met at Dunn's but had gone on to marry other people. Unfortunately, both of their spouses had passed away, but on the brighter side, they re-kindled their old relationship, married, and were attending their first dance in decades at Dunn's as a couple. It was very touching."

Will the Party Last?

They originally came to Dunn's to see the Big Bands, and today they're still coming to The Kee. Sure, the music has changed, but so has everything else in the world. When Gerry opened his hall we were in the middle of World War II. Since then the world has seen other wars, assassinations, natural disasters, musical trends, good times, bad times.....it's called life. And it continues. Just like the hall that Gerry built continues.

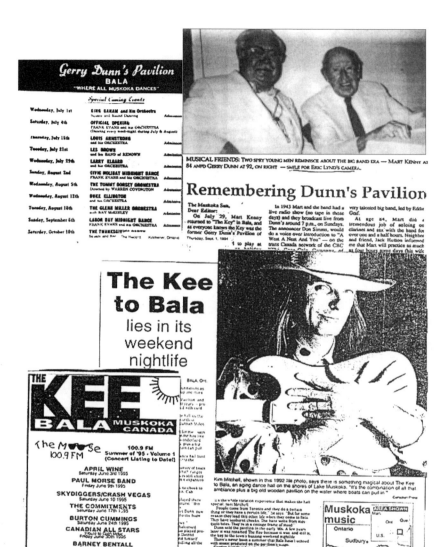

Mart Kenney pleased his generation of music fans in Bala and Kim Mitchell
continues this tradition

We've got posters !!

It's just a building. But oh, what a building it has been. Most of the hundreds of thousands of people who have entered this building can likely recall their own special thought or memory about their experience here. And it's not just the building itself that makes the memories - it's the people. Dunn's Pavilion/The Kee to Bala has been a conduit, bringing people together for one purpose, and that has been to meet, dance, enjoy music and have an evening of fun.

"It's the whole vacation experience that makes the hall special," perennial rock favourite Kim Mitchell recently told a newspaper reporter. "They're in a cottage frame of mind."

Gravenhurst resident Hugh Clairmont goes back further than Kim's generation, and so his comments to the same paper are perhaps a little more reflective of his generation. "I often think of the old days even today, the events we attended there (at Dunn's) and the people we met there years ago. It forms your character in life, the memories of that kind of thing."

About The Author

Peter Young is a freelance writer and runs his own communications company. Between 1963 and 1975 he played keyboards with a number of Toronto-based rock bands and travelled extensively throughout southern Ontario, performing in many of the province's popular dance pavilions including The Kee to Bala. He has recently completed a major book - "Come Dancing - A Celebration of Ontario's Dance Pavilions" - which  chronicles every well known dance pavilion and dancehall in the Province of Ontario. Most of these wonderful pavilions have disappeared due to fire, demolition or conversion to other uses. Peter has delved into the unique past of each pavilion, interviewing owners or their descendants, employees, the general public and also many of the musicians who performed at the various locations. His book, with its detailed text enhanced with dozens of photographs, portrays a human interest slice of Ontario's social and cultural history from the 1920's right up to the present, with much emphasis on the Big Band period of the 1930's to the '50's, as well as the rock 'n' roll years of the 1960's and '70's.

Young's book, "Come Dancing - A Celebration of Ontario's Dance Pavilions," (©1997 Peter Young) should be available soon. For more details on some of Ontario's musicians, Dunn's Pavilion/The Kee To Bala, or any other pavilion you recall with fond memories, you can write Peter c/o PDA Communications Ltd.

PHOTO CREDITS

P 3	P.Y. (Peter Young)
P 6	Bala Museum, P.Y.
P 8	Jack Lomas
P 10	Kay Thompson
P 11	Jack Lomas
P 14	Bala Museum
P 16	Marshall Louch
P 17	Marshall Louch, Don McIndoe
P 20	Don McIndoe
P 21	Marshall Louch
P 23	Jack Lomas
P 26	Don McIndoe, Pat McEachern
P 28	P.Y.
P 29	Don McIndoe (D.M.)
P 31	D.M.
P 37	D.M.
P 39	D.M.
P 40	D.M.
P 41	D.M.
P 42	D.M.
P 43	D.M.
P 44	D.M.
P 47	D.M.
P 52	P.Y.
P 54	P.Y.
P 60	P.Y.
P 61	D.M., Joe Kondyjowski
P 62	P.Y.
P 65	P.Y.

PUT THIS BOOK ON YOUR GIFT LIST!

Thanks for purchasing *The Kee To Bala Is Dunn`s Pavilion* - I hope you enjoyed reading about Muskoka`s celebrated dance pavilion and the significance it holds for so many people. If you would like to order additional copies as gifts for friends or relatives, please use this handy form below:

TO ORDER COPIES:

Yes, I would like to order _____ copies of *The Kee To Bala Is Dunn's Pavilion* @ $14.95 per copy plus $1.05 shipping and handling (Total $16.00). I have enclosed a cheque or money order made out to PDA Communications Ltd. for $ _____.

Name ....

Address ....

    ....

Province .... Postal Code ....

Please send this form to:
  PDA Communications Ltd.
  76 Hillcroft Street
  Oshawa, Ontario L1G 2L2
  Tel: Oshawa (905) 725-2954

Printed in Canada at Coach House Printing on bpNichol Lane.